Sparkle
and SHINE!

Trendy Earrings, Necklaces, and Hair Accessories for All Occasions

by Kara L. Laughlin

CAPSTONE PRESS
a capstone imprint

Savvy books are published by Capstone,
1710 Roe Crest Drive,
North Mankato, Minnesota 56003.

www.mycapstone.com

For information regarding permission, write to Capstone,
1710 Roe Crest Drive, North Mankato, Minnesota 56003.

Library of Congress Cataloging-in-Publication Data
Names: Laughlin, Kara L., author.
Title: Sparkle and shine! : trendy earrings, necklaces, and hair accessories for all
   occasions / by Kara L. Laughlin.
Description: North Mankato, Minnesota : Capstone Press, a Capstone imprint, [2017]
   | Series: Savvy. Accessorize yourself | Audience: Ages 9-13. | Audience: Grade 4 to 6. |
Includes bibliographical references and index.
Identifiers: LCCN 2016007069 | ISBN 9781491482285 (library binding) | ISBN
   9781491486184 (eBook PDF)
Subjects: LCSH: Jewelry making—Juvenile literature. | Handicraft for girls—Juvenile
   literature.
Classification: LCC TT212.L38 2017 | DDC 745.594/2—dc23
LC record available at https://lccn.loc.gov/2016007069

Editors: Mari Bolte and Alesha Halvorson
Designer: Tracy Davies McCabe
Project Creators: Marcy Morin, Sarah Schuette, and Lori Blackwell
Art Director: Heather Kindseth
Media Researcher: Morgan Walters
Premedia Specialist: Kathy McColley

Photo Credits:
All photos by Capstone Press: Karon Dubke

Artistic Effects:
Shutterstock: ganpanjanee, design element, Ozerina Anna,
design element, Stephanie Zieber, design element, Vaclav
Mach, design element, Yellowj, design element

Printed and bound in Canada.
009650F16

Table of
CONTENTS

YOU'RE *one of a kind,*

AND YOUR ACCESSORIES SHOULD BE TOO.

27

Cross-Purpose NECKLACE

One secret to great jewelry design: multiples! Tiles used for laying ceramic tiles. One spacer by itself may not look like much. But link them together with some colored cord, and you've crowd-sourced a beautiful necklace.

1. Use permanent markers or nail polish to color the tile spacers as desired.
2. Wrap a piece of beading cord around a spacer to make a small X in the center. Secure by tying the ends together in the center of the X. If using spacers of different sizes, try alternating them, or stacking smaller spacers on larger spacers.
3. Cut the tails off of each knot, and then dot with a dab of glue. Make sure the tails don't show from the front.
4. Tie one piece of the toggle clasp to the 22-inch beading cord. Thread a needle onto the other end.
5. Slip the needle beneath the wrapped cord on the back of a tile spacer. Slide the tile spacer to about ½ inch (1.3 cm) away from the toggle. Tie it in place.
6. Continue stringing tile spacers onto the necklace and tying them in place. Alternate

Really ROSY

These delicate rose earrings look intricate, but they are surprisingly simple to make. Use them to add a bit of understated style to a T-shirt and jeans. Pair them with an updo and a strappy dress for a special night out.

1. Knead a marble-sized piece of polymer clay until soft.
2. Break the clay into 16 equal balls.
3. Press one ball into a flat disk. Gently roll this disk up to make the central spiral of your rose.
4. Flatten another ball and curl it around the spiral.
5. Add six more petals to your rose. Always add in the same direction, and overlap the petals.
6. Repeat steps 3 through 5 to make a second rose.
7. Carefully cut the bottom of each rose to make it sit flat.
8. Set the roses onto a foil-lined baking sheet. Cure your roses in the oven according to package instructions.
9. When your roses have cooled completely, glue them to earring posts.

Tip: Now that you can make clay roses, add a matching bracelet! Make 8 to 12 roses, but before you bake them, press closed jump rings into opposite sides of each rose. Connect the roses with more jump rings and add a clasp.

MATERIALS:
polymer clay
baking them
jewelry glue
earring posts

35

YOU DON'T HAVE TO SPEND A MILLION BUCKS TO LOOK YOUR BEST.

With a little craft store swag and tools from around the house, you can make stylish accessories that turn heads without emptying your wallet.

You'll need a few tools if you're going to make jewelry at home. You may already have many of them. Others you may need to buy or borrow. But don't worry if you don't have a supply in your toolbox. Everything you need for these projects can be found at a craft store, home store, or online.

1. flat-nosed pliers
2. round-nosed pliers
3. chain-nosed pliers
4. crimping pliers
5. wire cutter
6. scissors
7. sewing needle
8. beading needle
9. hammer (for hardening metal)
10. paintbrushes
11. jewelry glue
12. jump rings (open and closed)
13. clasps
14. findings
15. crimp beads
16. head pins
17. eye pins
18. jewelry hand drill

From Drink TO 'DO

Did you know that most disposable drinking cups are made from shrinkable plastic? It's true! So the next time you're at a picnic or pool party, bring home your cup. No one will ever believe your latest accessory started as a drink holder!

MATERIALS:

parchment paper
baking sheet
red #6 plastic cup
permanent markers
hole punch

scissors
empty 16-ounce
   (0.5-liter) jar
bamboo skewer

Tip: Use small, 1-ounce (29.6-milliliter) cups to make a barrette version of this project.

1. Preheat oven to 250 degrees Fahrenheit (120 degrees Celsius). Lay a piece of parchment paper on a baking sheet.

2. Draw a fun design on the sides of your cup with permanent markers.

3. Punch two holes on opposite sides of the cup about ½ inch (1.3 centimeters) from the rim.

4. Carefully cut away the bottom of the cup.

5. Set the cup bottom up on the parchment paper and put it in the oven.

6. The cup will collapse into a puffy disk in 3 to 5 minutes. As soon as it does, remove it from the oven. Use a potholder to curve it around the sides of your jar.

7. Trim your bamboo skewer to 6 inches (15.2 cm).

8. Once the cup has cooled, slide the skewer though the holes. (You may need to re-punch the holes.)

MATERIALS:

scissors
stiffened craft felt
hair comb
vintage buttons
  and jewelry

felt glue
needle and clear nylon
  thread or fishing line

Vintage GLAMOUR

A few pieces of old costume jewelry or vintage buttons can transform hair combs from blah to bling. Search thrift stores and yard sales for your finds. Limit choices to one or two main colors to keep the project glam, not gaudy.

5

Tip: If combs don't work well in your hair, decorate a headband instead. Sew a loop of elastic to the back of the felt and slide it onto a plastic headband. You can keep it removable or glue it in place.

1. Cut a piece of stiffened felt the same length as your hair comb.

2. Arrange buttons and jewelry pieces in a pattern on the felt. Use felt glue to glue into place. Let dry.

3. Cut away the extra felt from around the buttons and jewelry pieces.

4. Thread needle with thread or fishing line and secure the knot with felt glue.

5. Sew the felt to the comb by wrapping the thread around the top of the comb. Sew all the way across the comb and back to make sure the felt is secure. Knot the thread and cut off any excess.

6. Lay down a line of felt glue where the felt meets the top of the comb. Let the glue dry before wearing.

MATERIALS:

serrated knife
plastic bottle with long neck
scissors
ponytail holder
sandpaper

decoupage glue
    and paintbrush
fabric
sticky-back pearls

Rockin' HAIR CUFF

*Sometimes you want to rock a more polished pony.
Enter this hair cuff. It's great for casual hair days
when you want to keep a little edge.*

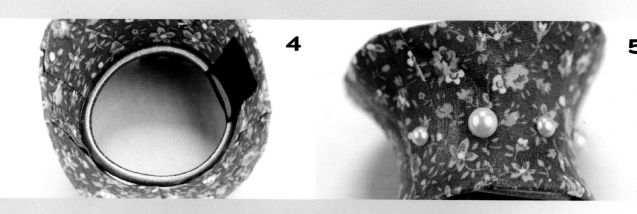

1. Use a serrated knife to cut a 2-inch (5-cm) tube from the bottle's neck.

2. Use scissors to make a cut down the length of one side of the tube.

3. Lightly sand the outside of the tube. Add a thin layer of decoupage glue. Press fabric into the glue to cover the tube and trim off excess. Brush more decoupage over the top of the fabric. Let dry completely.

4. Secure a ponytail holder to the inside of the tube with a piece of electrical tape. Cover the tape with more fabric and decoupage.

5. Add sticky-back pearls to the cuff.

6. To use your hair cuff, gather your hair into a ponytail and slip the ponytail holder over your hair. Position the cuff so that the top sits close to your scalp. Secure the ponytail holder normally.

*Tip: If you're more punk than rock, cover the tube with electric tape
and decorate with metal screw brads or grommets.*

Boho Bling HAIRBAND

Turban-style hair wraps are super comfy and look great. This one adds to the swag factor with a sparkly chain and fabric you dye yourself.

MATERIALS:

tape measure
wire cutter
metal chain
beaded chain
scissors

knit cotton fabric
craft glue
no-boil fabric dye
needle and thread

> *Tip: Don't use the stovetop method to dye the fabric. It could melt the glue.*

1. Measure the widest part of your head. Use the wire cutter to cut the metal and beaded chains to this measurement. Then cut a piece of cotton fabric, using the measurement for the length and 5 inches (12.7 cm) for the width.

2. Spread the fabric out on a work surface and squeeze glue in a fun pattern onto the cloth. Let the glue dry overnight.

3. Dye your cloth according to the package instructions. If some fabric puffs up while you're dying, use a wooden spoon or butter knife to push the air pocket to the edge of the fabric. That should release the bubble and let the fabric sink back into the dye. When your fabric is dyed and rinsed, but still damp, peel off the glue.

4. Wash the fabric and let it dry completely before sewing.

5. Fold your fabric along its length so that the right side of the pattern is on the inside. Sew the edges together lengthwise to make a tube. Turn the tube right-side-out.

6. Lay the chains on the fabric in an X. Sew them to the fabric where the chains cross. Sew the ends of the chains to the ends of the fabric ½ inch (1.3 cm) from the raw edges of the fabric.

7. Tuck ½ inch (1.3 cm) of one side of the tube into the other. Fold the outside fabric about ¼ inch (0.6 cm) under and sew the fabric together to make a circle.

MATERIALS:

sharp knife
chopsticks or natural twigs
sandpaper
vegetable or coconut oil
clean cloth or paper towel

20-guage wire
pearl beads
wire cutter
eye screw
jump ring

Hair Sticks TO GO

Use take-out to take back fashion! These hair sticks will help rein in your locks when you're letting your inner wild child come out to play.

1. Use a sharp knife to whittle a gentle point (about the shape of a dull pencil) at one end of a chopstick or stick. If using natural twigs, set them aside to dry until they are hard and strong, about three days.

2. Carve a notch into the blunt end of one stick about ¼ inch (0.6 cm) from the end.

3. Sand the sticks. Then rub oil over them with a clean cloth or paper towel.

4. Wrap wire around the notch of one stick, and then twist together to secure. Add three beads to the wire. Twist to secure the beads in a triangle at the top of the hair stick.

5. Cut the wire and weave the ends in and around the beads in a bowl shape. Wrap the ends of the wire around the notch again to secure the nest to the stick.

6. Twist an eye screw into the other stick. Attach the center of your chain to the eye screw with a jump ring.

7. Use a jump ring to attach charms to each end of the chain.

HOW TO WHITTLE

Whittling is a fun and safe activity as long as you take a couple of precautions.

- Check your "circle of safety" to make sure no one is around: Hold your knife at arm's length and bring it around your body and over your head.
- Use a sharp knife. Dull knives are more likely to slip and cut you.
- Always cut away from your body.
- Don't rush! Lots of little shavings will work better than deep cuts.

Punchy Puff HEADBAND

Who knew paper could be this pretty—and strong?
This is a great everyday headband for when you
want to just add a little punch to your 'do.

3

MATERIALS:

large cooking pot
serrated knife or craft saw
5-inch (12.7-cm) wooden
   embroidery hoop
bowl or jar, about 4 inches
   (10.2 cm) wide
flower-shaped paper punch

scrapbooking paper in several
   contrasting colors
1 inch (2.5 cm) round
   paper punch
½-inch (1.3-cm) round
   paper punch
dimensional decoupage glue

1. Fill the pot about halfway with water. Then bring the water to a boil.

2. Cut the metal parts off of the outer ring of the embroidery hoop. Boil the hoop in the water until it's flexible, about 20 minutes.

3. Use tongs to remove hoop from the water and rinse it in cold water until it's cool enough to handle. Bend the hoop and place the ends in the bowl or jar. Leave the hoop in the bowl until it's completely dry. This could take several hours, or even overnight.

4. Punch 6 flowers from each sheet of scrapbooking paper. Set the flowers on a protected work surface. Cover the flowers with dimensional decoupage.

5. Repeat step 4 with the round paper punches. Cover the circles with dimensional decoupage. Let the flowers and the circles dry completely.

6. Use decoupage glue to attach the larger circles to the flowers, and the flowers and smaller circles to the headband. Use additional glue along the underside of the flowers for added stability. Let dry completely.

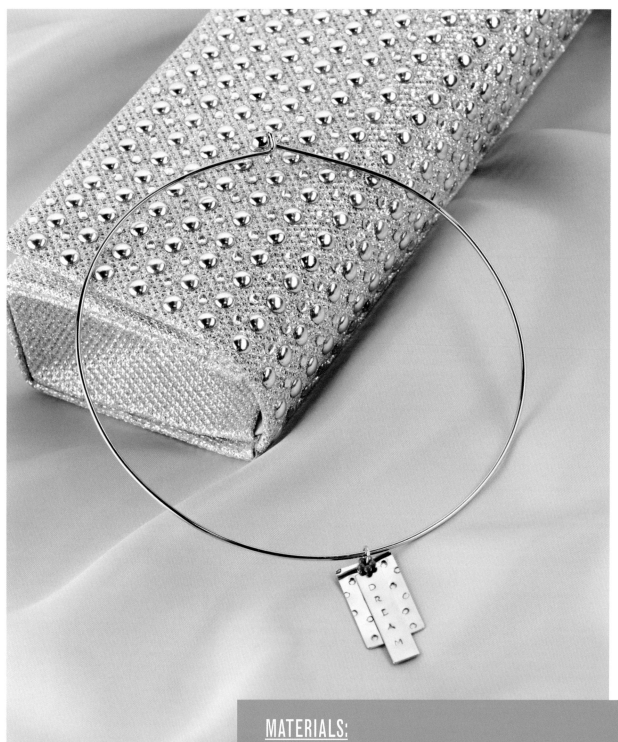

MATERIALS:

metal blanks with
    beading holes
pencil
stamping block or flat
    piece of metal

alphabet metal stamping kit
hammer
jump ring
small bead
metal choker necklace

Make Your MARK

Metal stamping is easier than you think! A set of stamps, a few swings of your hammer, and you've got a personalized pendant. When you see how easy they are, you'll be making them for all of your friends.

3

Tips: Practice makes perfect! Experiment with a throwaway blank before diving in.

Stamping kits and blanks can be found at craft stores. Check sales and use store coupons to get the best deals.

1. Lightly mark the metal blank with a pencil to make sure your letters will be centered and evenly spaced. If your blanks are small, a piece or two of clear tape along the edges can help keep the blanks in place.

2. Stamp your design onto the blank. Hold the stamp straight over the blank. Hold the hammer near the head, and gently hammer the stamp once.

3. Continue stamping until the blank is decorated to your liking. Use a damp rag to rub off the pencil marks from step 1.

4. Thread the bead onto the jump ring. Then thread the metal blank onto the jump ring.

5. Hang your stamped charm off the metal choker necklace.

MATERIALS:

1-inch (2.5-cm) circle
    paper punch
playing cards
scissors
embossing fluid
metallic embossing powder
paintbrush

hair dryer
pushpin
clear nail polish
jewelry pliers
jump rings
12-inch (30.5-cm) piece
    of necklace chain

Dealing Up DESIGN

The next time you discover a few cards missing from your favorite deck, don't toss the rest. Show off the detailed designs by incorporating them into this scalloped necklace.

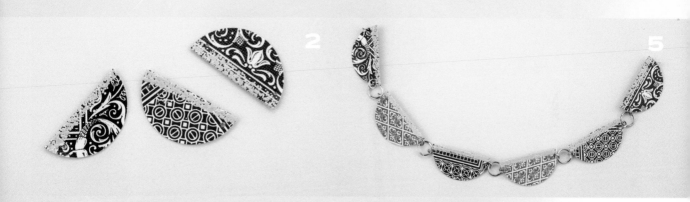

1. Punch 8 circles from playing cards. Then cut them in half.

2. Pour embossing fluid onto a paper plate. Dip the cut edges of the half circles into the fluid. Then dip the edges with embossing powder. Use a dry paintbrush to dust off any excess powder. Heat the powder with a hair dryer until the powder melts and turns shiny.

3. Use a pushpin to poke a hole in each of the top corners of the card pieces. Add a drop of clear nail polish to each hole. Let dry.

4. Use jewelry pliers to thread a jump ring through one of the holes. Use the jump rings to join 10 card pieces.

5. Repeat to make a second chain of six card pieces. Attach the ends of the chains to one another.

6. Attach the necklace chain to the jump rings at the ends of the card pieces.

Tip: Open and close those jump rings right! Use two pairs of pliers and twist the ends perpendicular to the ring. When you twist back to close, wobbling the ends will help keep it closed.

MATERIALS:

craft glue
pendant with bezel setting
foil-lined seed beads, size 12
tweezers
loose seed beads

sponge
powdered tile grout or
   mosaic grout
decorative chain or string
   of seed beads with a clasp

Magical MOSAIC

Don't you just love it when all the little things come together? Foil-lined beads make this pendant sparkle, and mosaic grout keeps them in place.

Tip: *If you don't have grout handy, you can use clear resin. Be sure to pop any air bubbles before you let the resin dry.*

1. Use glue to draw a shape on the inside of the bezel setting.

2. Lay your beads on the glue. Use tweezers to nudge the string into a smooth shape. Let the glue dry.

3. Remove the excess beads from your design. Fill the rest of the bezel setting with glue, and add loose beads in a second color to cover the rest of the bezel setting. Let dry.

4. Follow package instructions to mix grout. Apply grout evenly to the beads. It's okay if the beads don't show through or look dusty.

5. Allow the grout to dry for one hour. Wipe off excess grout with a damp sponge.

6. Let grout set for another day, then wipe again with a damp sponge.

7. Hang the pendant on a chain or string of beads.

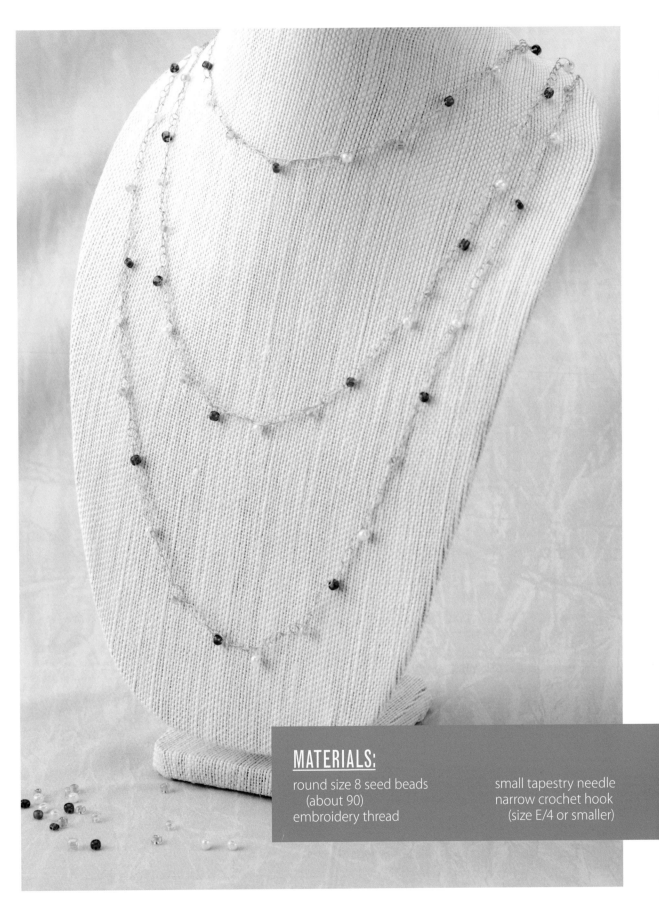

MATERIALS:

round size 8 seed beads
(about 90)
embroidery thread

small tapestry needle
narrow crochet hook
(size E/4 or smaller)

Beauty and the BEADS

Wear this fiber necklace long, or wrap it around your neck a few times for a layered look. It's amazing how pretty slipping one loop over another can be—when you do it several hundred times!

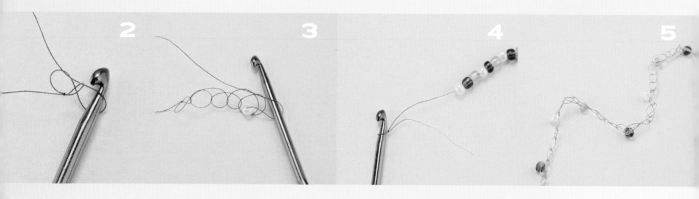

1. Thread beads onto your spool of embroidery thread with your beading needle.

2. Tie a loop in the end of the thread, and put the loop on your crochet hook.

3. Twist thread around your crochet hook and slip the first loop off of the hook. This is a single crochet.

4. After five single crochets, push a bead up so that it gets wrapped around the hook. When you slip the loop off the hook, slip the loop over the bead as well.

5. Continue making single crochets, and adding a bead every fifth stitch, until the necklace measures 48 inches (122 cm).

6. Slip the hook back into the beginning of your chain. Wrap the hook as usual, and then slip both loops off of hook. Cut the thread away from the spool and pull the end through.

7. With your tapestry needle, weave the end of the thread back into the necklace.

Tip: Get a very different look with different materials. Try using satin or organza ribbon with ¼ inch (0.6 cm) painted glass beads for a more romantic look. You can even crochet a chain from beading wire.

MATERIALS:

permanent markers or nail polish
  in various colors
X-shaped tile spacers
beading cord
clear glue

toggle clasp
22-inch- (56-cm-) long piece
  of beading cord
tapestry needle
beads of various sizes

Cross-Purpose NECKLACE

One secret to great jewelry design: multiples! Tile spacers are used for laying ceramic tiles. One spacer by itself may not look like much. But link them together with some colored cord, and you've crowd-sourced a beautiful necklace.

1. Use permanent markers or nail polish to color the tile spacers as desired.

2. Wrap a piece of beading cord around a spacer to make a small X in the center. Secure by tying the ends together in the center of the X. If using spacers of different sizes, try alternating them, or stacking smaller spacers on larger spacers.

3. Cut the tails off of each knot, and then dot with a dab of glue. Make sure the tails don't show from the front.

4. Tie one piece of the toggle clasp to the 22-inch beading cord. Thread a needle onto the other end.

5. Slip the needle beneath the wrapped cord on the back of a tile spacer. Slide the tile spacer to about ½ inch (1.3 cm) away from the toggle. Tie it in place.

6. Continue stringing tile spacers onto the necklace and tying them in place. Alternate with beads, if desired.

7. Tie the end of the cord to the second part of the toggle clasp. Cut off ends and glue the clasp knots.

Tip: Tying knots gets tricky when you've got a few crosses strung. To make it easier, let your needle do the work. After you've strung the tile space, slide your needle through the wrapped cord to make a loop. Slip the needle through the loop, and then pull tight to knot your tile spacer in place.

small lock charm
48-inch (122-cm) chain with
   round links at least ⅜ inch
   (0.1 cm) in diameter

¼-inch- (0.6-cm-) wide
   leather cord
coordinating key charm
two ¼-inch beads

Lariat Lock DOWN

This lariat necklace is key to having a little versatility in your jewelry wardrobe. Since it adjusts to any neckline, you'll always have a lock on a great look.

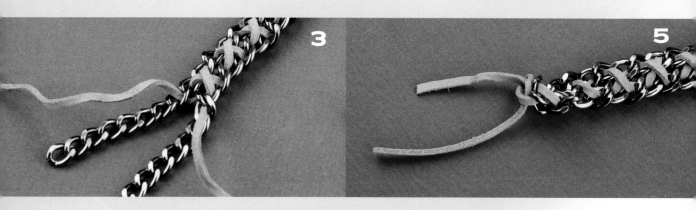

1. Slip the lock charm onto the chain and fold the chain so that the ends are together with the lock hanging at the other end.

2. Cut an 8-foot (2.4-meter) piece of cord. Starting at the lock end, thread the cord through links on either side of the chain. Even out the cord so that both ends are the same length.

3. Thread the left cord down through the next open link on the right chain. Then thread the right cord down the next open link on the left chain.

4. Your cord should be on the underside of the chain. Cross the cords and send them back up through the next links.

5. Continue lacing the cord through the chain all the way down. Tie a knot, but do not cut the ends.

6. Slip the working end of the chain through the lock's handle. Then tie the key to the working end of the chain.

7. Tie a bead to the end of each cord, then cut off the end.

MATERIALS:

polymer clay
drinking straws cut into
    3-inch (7.6-cm) pieces
aluminum foil
baking sheet
scissors
20-inch- (51-cm-) long chain

20-inch- (51-cm-) long piece of
    ½-inch-(1.3-cm-) wide ribbon
4 ribbon crimps
14-mm jump rings
necklace clasp
pendant

In a TWIST

Here's a new twist on a romantic ribbon necklace.
The handmade spiral beads add a splash of color and
fun—perfect for a night out with friends.

1. Pull off a marble-sized piece of polymer clay, and knead it until it's soft.

2. Roll the clay into a snake about ¼-inch (0.6-cm) in diameter. Wrap the snake in a tight spiral around a drinking straw, and set onto a foil-lined baking sheet.

3. Repeat steps 1 and 2 to make three more beads.

4. Bake the clay beads according to the package instructions.

5. When the beads have baked and cooled, slide them off of the straws.

6. Gather the two ribbons and chain together. Insert them into the top of a spiral bead. Twist the spiral around the ribbon and chain until they are completely inside the spiral. Add the rest of your beads the same way.

7. Add a ribbon crimp to each of your ribbon ends.

8. Attach the ribbon crimps and chain to your clasp with a jump ring. Use another jump ring to attach the pendant.

Tip: These beads work well alone too! Before you cure them, make loops in the ends for jump rings. You can cluster five or seven together for a squiggly pendant, or link them together lengthwise for a fun bracelet.

Edgy EAR CUFF

Ear cuffs give you the look of a piercing without being permanent. Next time you want to add a little edge to your look, slip this on and rock out.

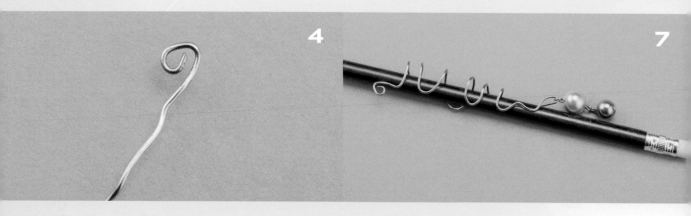

1. Using jewelry pliers, bend the copper wire in half.

2. About 1 ½ inches (3.8 cm) from the first bend, bend the wire back in the other direction. Repeat on the other side.

3. Make two more bends, about 1 inch (2.5 cm) farther down the wire on each side. The wire should look like a tight zigzag with long ends.

4. About 1 inch beyond the last bends, bend the end of the wire at a 90-degree angle. On the left side, shape the wire into a spiral.

5. Make two soft bends in the left side of the wire. Use round-nosed pliers to make a loop at the end.

6. Thread your bead on a head pin. Curl the head pin closed around the wire loop.

7. Bend the five prongs of the zigzag up and around a pencil.

8. Fit your ear cuff around the top of your ear, making sure the spiral and the drop bead are visible from the front.

Tip: Everyone's body is different, and that goes for ears too! If your cuff is too loose or too tight, you may need to start over and adjust the length of wire between the hairpin bends. Or you may want to try a thinner wire (20-gauge).

MATERIALS:

polymer clay
penknife
aluminum foil

baking sheet
jewelry glue
earring posts

Really ROSY

These delicate rose earrings look intricate, but they are surprisingly simple to make. Use them to add a bit of understated style to a T-shirt and jeans. Pair them with an updo and a strappy dress for a special night out.

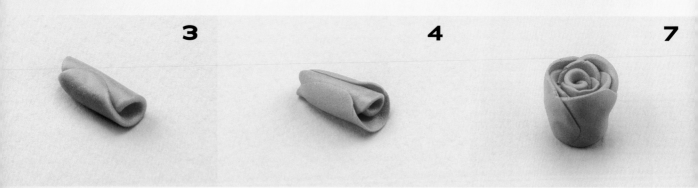

3   **4**   **7**

1. Knead a marble-sized piece of polymer clay until soft.

2. Break the clay into 16 equal balls.

3. Press one ball into a flat disk. Gently roll this disk up to make the central spiral of your rose.

4. Flatten another ball and curl it around the spiral.

5. Add six more petals to your rose. Always add in the same direction, and overlap the petals.

6. Repeat steps 3–5 to make a second rose.

7. Carefully cut the bottom of each rose to make it sit flat.

8. Set the roses onto a foil-lined baking sheet. Cure your roses in the oven according to package instructions.

9. When your roses have cooled completely, glue them to earring posts.

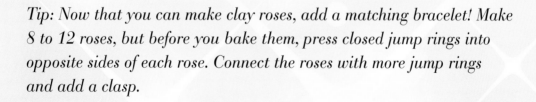

Tip: Now that you can make clay roses, add a matching bracelet! Make 8 to 12 roses, but before you bake them, press closed jump rings into opposite sides of each rose. Connect the roses with more jump rings and add a clasp.

MATERIALS:

16 to 20 thin gauge (8- to 12-mm) jump rings

two 1-inch- (2.5-cm-) long pieces of brass chain, ⅛ inch (0.3 cm) in diameter

two 1 ½-inch- (3.8 cm-) long pieces of brass chain, ⅛ inch (0.3 cm) in diameter

two 2 ½-inch- (6.4 cm-) long pieces of silver chains, ¼ inch (0.6-cm) in diameter

four 1 ¼-inch- (3.2 cm-) long peices of silver chain, ⅛ (0.3 cm) inch in diameter

two 1 ¼-inch- (3.2 cm-) long pieces of copper chain, ¼ inch (0.6 cm) in diameter

two 2-inch- (5-cm-) long pieces of copper chain, ¼ (0.6 cm) inch in diameter

two 2-inch-long pieces of copper chain, ⅛ inch (0.3 cm) in diameter

two 1 ½ inch-long pieces of copper chain, ⅛ inch (0.3 cm) in diameter

two pairs jewelry pliers

6 top-drilled crystal teardrop beads

ear wires

Crystal CHANDELIERS

*When your outfit calls for high drama, break out
these chandelier earrings. The mixed metals mean
you can wear them with most fashion styles.
Bonus: they're a great way to upcycle old necklaces.*

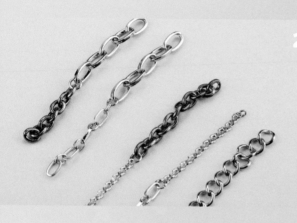 

1. Use a jump ring to attach a 1-inch- (2.5-cm-) long piece of brass chain to a 1 ¼-inch (3.2-cm) piece of silver chain.

2. Repeat to attach a 1 ¼-inch- (3.2-cm-) long piece of silver chain with a matching piece of copper chain. Make pairs of 1 ½-inch chain and 2-inch (5-cm) chain in the same way.

3. Arrange your chain pairs so that the shorter pieces are on the outside and the longer ones are in the center. You will have one 2 ½-inch (6.4-cm) piece of silver chain in the center.

4. Use the jump ring to attach the chains to the earring through the holes on the bottom.

5. Thread a jump ring through one of the crystal beads. Attach the bead to the bottom of the longest chain. Attach two more crystal beads to the next longest chains.

6. Hang your earring on the loop at the bottom of the ear wire. Use pliers to close up the loop.

7. Repeat steps 1–7 to make a second earring.

*Tip: For a retro look, skip the crystals and paint the
chains with brightly colored nail polish or enamel paint.*

Ten-Minute HOOPS

Hoops are the blue jeans of jewelry—you can wear them every day, and they go with anything. Make a few pairs with different beads, and you'll always have something to wear with your favorite outfits.

4

1. Wrap a piece of wire completely around the spool one time. Add ½ inch (1.3 cm), then cut.

2. With a round-nosed pliers, turn the extra half inch of wire into a loop.

3. Grasp the loop with a flat-nosed pliers and bend it away from the hoop at a 45-degree angle. Set aside.

4. Thread a head pin through one of the large beads. Use round-nosed pliers to make a loop at the top of the head pin.

5. String four seed beads onto the hoop. Add the large bead. Then string four more seed beads.

6. Use the flat-nosed pliers to bend up the free end of the hoop. Trim off any extra wire and smooth the cut end with a nail file.

7. Gently hammer each side of the hoop flat.

8. Repeat steps 1–7 for the second earring.

TEMPER, TEMPER!

Wire has to be bendy enough to work with, but not so bendy that it loses its shape. Fortunately, there's a way to have your wire flexible when you're working it, and firm when you finish. It's called tempering.

Here are a few ways to temper your jewelry wire:

• pull the wire straight with nylon-nosed pliers

• bend it as you work with it

• hammer it

Be careful! If you work the metal too much, it becomes brittle and can break.

MATERIALS:

wool roving in two colors
hot water
dish soap
needle that will fit through the
　holes in your beads

thread
seed beads
closed jump rings
ear wires

Felting FUN

When you think of wool, you probably think sweaters or socks. But wool is great for jewelry too. It's strong, inexpensive, and easy to decorate. These earrings start off as little more than fluff. With a little work, though, you'll have bits of felt perfect for fashion.

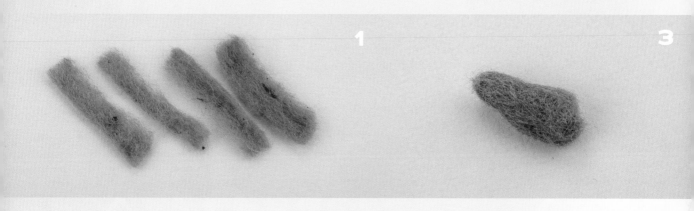

1. Pull four to five pieces of wool roving into a strip about 3 inches (7.6 cm) by ½ inch (1.3 cm). Tie the wool into a loose knot.

2. Dip the wool in hot, soapy water. Roll the knot around in your hands for about 15 minutes, until it's tight and round.

3. Pull about twice as much roving as before and dip it in the water. Make a long teardrop shape by gently rolling the wool back and forth.

4. Repeat steps 1–3 for the second earring. Allow felted pieces to dry for two days.

5. Sew seed beads onto the felt pieces.

6. Attach closed jump rings to the top and bottom of each felt ball.

7. Sew each teardrop to the bottom jump rings. Attach earring wires to the top jump rings.

Tip: If your wool shapes keep breaking open, start over with a new piece of roving and be gentler when you roll it. Too much pressure will felt the piece before it has time to knit together into the shape that you want.

MATERIALS:

nail polish in two
    contrasting colors
4 lock washers, ½ inch
    (1.3 cm) in diameter

beads
silk or nylon beading
    cord and needle
ear wires

Sunburst DANGLES

Jewelry supplies don't just come from the craft store. These earrings are made of lock washers, found at hardware and home improvement stores. Make these baubles bright with a pop of color and a few pretty beads.

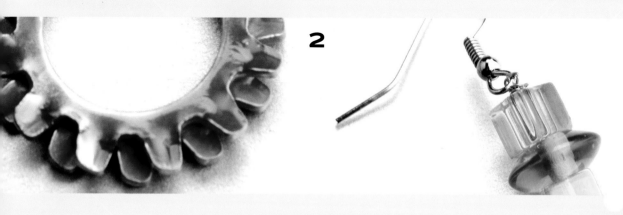

1. Use nail polish to paint one pair of washers. Paint the second pair of washers with the second color. Let dry.

2. Position one lock washer over another of the other color. Their prongs should alternate to make a two-color starburst shape.

3. Fold an 18-inch (45.7-cm) piece of beading cord in half. Slip the center through one pair of lock washers, and then pass the ends through to make a slipknot.

4. Tie one end of the cord to the needle. Thread three beads onto the cord, then pass the needle through an ear wire. Send the needle back down through the beads and tie it to the other end of the beading cord.

5. Send the needle back up through the beads, and cut the cord between two beads so that the end disappears between them.

6. Thread the other end of the beading cord and hide its end between the beads in the same way.

7. Repeat for the second earring, alternating which color washer is on top, if desired.

SOURCING OUTSIDE THE BOX

Hardware stores aren't the only places hiding jewelry equipment in plain sight! Next time you're in one of these stores, keep a lookout for these great components:

hardware store: washers, nuts, zip ties, fan pulls, tile spacers, tile grout, bungee cords, keys, chains

office supply store: metal brads, paper clips, metal and paper price tags, pencils, safety pins

fabric store: zippers, buttons, buckles, plastic cord guide rings, ribbons, fringe, tassels

electronics store: resistors, LED lights, copper wire, electrical tape, PVC tape

Quirky Cork POSTS

Slices of cork are the perfect canvases for rubber stamps and ink. These earrings are so adaptable, you could make several pairs with completely different looks.

MATERIALS:

cork bottle stopper
serrated knife
alcohol ink
patterned rubber stamp
   and stamp pad
permanent markers
tissue paper
decoupage glue

two ¼-inch (0.6-cm)
   eye screws or head pins
jewelry glue
2 round or oval beads
2 eye pins
round-nosed pliers
earring posts and backs

4

1. Cut two ⅛-inch- (0.3-cm-) thick pieces of cork with a serrated knife.

2. Add a drop of alcohol ink to two or three places on the cork disks. Let dry.

3. Ink your rubber stamp and press it onto the cork so that the top half of the cork is covered in the pattern. Use permanent markers to color in the pattern on the cork, if desired.

4. Tear two pieces of tissue paper into 1 inch (2.5 cm) squares. Lay the tissue paper across the bottom halves of the corks. Paint the paper with decoupage glue and wrap the edges around the cork. Let dry.

5. Gently twist eye screws into the bottom edges of the cork disks. Secure with a dot of jewelry glue.

6. Thread beads onto the eye pins. Use round-nosed pliers to loop them through the eye screw.

7. Secure earring posts to the backs of the cork circles with jewelry glue.

MATERIALS:

alcohol inks in two colors
2 metal blanks with a hole
   at the top
cotton swabs
jump rings
ear wires

chandelier findings with
   three links
14 ⅛-inch (0.3-cm) beads
14 head pins
round-nosed pliers

Rainy Day DANGLES

Need a lift on a gray day? Try on some fab earrings!
The back disks of these earrings may look like puddles in
the rain, but with these pretty dangles in your ears, you'll
be walking on sunshine all day long.

2

6

1. Place one drop of alcohol ink onto each blank. Add one or two drops of the other color. Use a cotton swab to push the ink around on the metal. When you have the look you want, let it dry.

2. Attach a jump ring to the top of a blank.

3. Thread an earring wire and a chandelier finding onto the jump ring. Thread another jump ring onto the chandelier finding.

4. Place a bead on a head pin, then use the pliers to close the head pin. Repeat to make six more beads.

5. Hang one bead off the jump ring from step 2. Add three more beads to the second jump ring.

6. Use more jump rings to hang a bead onto each of the chandelier finding's links.

Read More

Berne, Emma Carlson. *Jewelry Tips & Tricks*. Style Secrets.
Minneapolis: Lerner Publications, 2016.

Lim, Annalees. *Jewelry Crafts*. Craft Attack!
New York: Gareth Stevens Publishing, 2014.

Reid, Emily. *I Can Make Jewelry*. Makerspace Projects.
New York: Windmill Books, 2016.

About the Author

Kara Laughlin is the author of more than two dozen books for kids. When she isn't writing, she spends her time making embroidered jewelry and teaching kids about writing, making things, and the natural world. She lives in Leesburg, Virginia, with her husband, three kids, one dog, and two guinea pigs.

Books in this series: